Free Video  Free Video

Essential Test Tips Video from Trivium Test Prep

Dear Customer,

Thank you for purchasing from Trivium Test Prep! We're honored to help you prepare for your GT exam.

To show our appreciation, we're offering a **FREE** *GT Essential Test Tips* **Video by Trivium Test Prep**.* Our video includes 35 test preparation strategies that will make you successful on the GT. All we ask is that you email us your feedback and describe your experience with our product. Amazing, awful, or just so-so: we want to hear what you have to say!

To receive your **FREE** *GT Essential Test Tips* **Video**, please email us at 5star@triviumtestprep.com. Include "Free 5 Star" in the subject line and the following information in your email:

1. The title of the product you purchased.
2. Your rating from 1 – 5 (with 5 being the best).
3. Your feedback about the product, including how our materials helped you meet your goals and ways in which we can improve our products.
4. Your full name and shipping address so we can send your **FREE** *GT Essential Test Tips* **Video**.

If you have any questions or concerns please feel free to contact us directly at 5star@triviumtestprep.com.

Thank you!

– Trivium Test Prep Team

*To get access to the free video please email us at 5star@triviumtestprep.com, and please follow the instructions above.

GIFTED AND TALENTED KINDERGARTEN WORKBOOK AND STUDY GUIDE:

Test Prep Material with Practice Questions for the CogAT Level 5/6, and OLSAT and NNAT Level A Exams

Jonathan Cox

Table of Contents

Introduction iii

PART I
Verbal Skills 1

ONE: Completing the
Sentence........................... 3

TWO: Picture
Analogies........................ 13

THREE: Comparing
Pictures (Similarities) 21

FOUR: Comparing
Pictures (Differences) 27

FIVE: Picture Series 33

PART II
Math Skills...................... 39

SIX: Number
Analogies........................ 41

SEVEN: Number
Puzzles 47

EIGHT: Number
Series 53

NINE: Arithmetic
Reasoning 59

PART III
Spatial Skills.................... 65

TEN: Comparing Figures
(Finding Similarities) 67

ELEVEN: Comparing
Figures (Finding
Differences)..................... 73

TWELVE: Figure
Analogies......................... 79

THIRTEEN: Paper
Folding 85

FOURTEEN: Pattern
Matrices.......................... 93

FIFTEEN: Pattern
Completion 99

SIXTEEN: Figure
Series 105

Introduction

Congratulations on your child's application for a gifted and talented program! By purchasing this book, you're helping your child take an important step toward academic success.

This guide will provide you with a detailed overview of the most common gifted and talented exams so that you know exactly what your child will see on test day. We'll take you through all the skills covered on the exam and help your child prepare with practice questions and fun activities.

We're pleased you've chosen Accepted, Inc., to be a part of your journey!

What Is Gifted and Talented Education?

GIFTED AND TALENTED (GT) PROGRAMS serve students whose talents and gifts are not fully met through traditional education programs. While federal legislation requires states to meet the needs of gifted students, it provides no specifics as to how this is best accomplished. For this reason, GT education programming varies from state to state and, in some cases, district to district and school to school. Some of the most common models for gifted education include the following:

- ▶ School-wide gifted and talented programming may be created by setting aside certain schools to serve the needs of gifted students. These schools are sometimes called GT magnet schools, vanguard schools, or by other names.

- ▶ Separate classes within the school specifically for gifted and talented students are another popular model. In this approach, a single school might have three kindergarten classes. Two will offer grade-level instruction, and one will offer specialized instruction for gifted and talented students.

- ▶ Additional programming for GT students as part of the school day is another model. In this model, students identified as gifted and talented receive additional programming either through a special "pull-out" class, or in some cases, a GT teacher will visit students in their main classroom to provide "push-in" programming.

- Modifications within the traditional classroom setting are also sometimes used. Most primary educators receive training in gifted and talented education. They are then able to extend and modify the core curriculum as needed for GT students. They might also use an additional supplemental curriculum with identified students or provide other types of enrichment activities.

Any particular school or district may use one of these models or multiple GT programming models. It is also worth noting that GT program options typically change as students advance in school. For example, gifted high school students may be adequately challenged through dual-credit college courses, AP courses, and other advanced classes.

Further, supplemental education programs from tutoring centers, private tutors, or online classes can provide more enrichment for gifted students in schools or districts without significant GT programming.

How Are Students Chosen for Gifted and Talented Programs?

There are no federal laws that mandate procedures for identification of gifted and talented students. Many school districts universally assess all students to screen for giftedness. Others provide the option for all students to participate in such testing at increments throughout their education or upon parent request.

Schools use multiple screening methods to identify giftedness. In some cases, a point rating system based on multiple criteria is used. While intelligence tests (like those described here) are common and almost always part of identification, they are not the only criteria for identification. Other common methods include:

- teacher recommendations/referrals
- parent/teacher checklists
- student work portfolios
- student interviews
- achievement test scores
- past student performance records (e.g., report cards)

What Kind of Test Will Students Take?

Standardized assessment measures for gifted education are designed to test students' cognitive development and compare that with the typical development of peers. They measure verbal/language skills, quantitative/number skills, and nonverbal reasoning.

The **COGNITIVE ABILITIES TEST (COGAT) LEVEL 5/6** test is administered to kindergarten students. It contains three sections:

- ▶ verbal battery (picture analogies, sentence completion, and picture classification)
- ▶ quantitative battery (number analogies, number series, number puzzles)
- ▶ nonverbal battery (figure matrices, figure classification, and paper folding)

It has a total of **118 QUESTIONS** and a total testing time of **112 MINUTES**. Each battery ranges from 20 – 45 minutes. However, the total testing time may be longer to allow time for directions to be read, etc.

The **OTIS–LENNON SCHOOL ABILITY TEST (OLSAT) LEVEL A** for kindergarten contains **40 QUESTIONS** and takes approximately **60 MINUTES**. It is divided into a verbal and a nonverbal section. The verbal section contains verbal comprehension and verbal reasoning questions. The nonverbal section contains pictorial reasoning, figural reasoning, and quantitative reasoning.

The **NAGLIERI NONVERBAL ABILITY TEST (NNAT) LEVEL A** exam contains **48 QUESTIONS** completed in **30 MINUTES**. It contains only nonverbal questions in the form of pattern completion and reasoning by analogy questions.

Each of the three exams makes use of pictorial illustrations as the primary means for assessment. Students will be presented with a series of pictures and will have to choose the one that best completes the series or answers the question. Students who are blind or who have significant visual impairments will typically be assessed through an alternate method.

CogAT is the only assessment that measures verbal, nonverbal, and quantitative skills. OLSAT measures both verbal and nonverbal skills. NNAT measures only nonverbal skills. Some schools might use only portions of the assessment—perhaps the verbal battery from OLSAT with the nonverbal assessment from NNAT. Because tests are broken into multiple batteries, it is not uncommon for a school to use one test for one battery and another test for another battery. Parents should ask which battery or batteries from which exams will be administered.

Scores from any of these three tests are most often used as part of qualification criteria for gifted and talented eligibility. Seldom are they used as the sole criteria. Further, it should be noted that such assessments are not without flaws, and some students with true giftedness are not properly identified through such methods because of a language barrier with the examiner, an underlying disability, or many other situations that may interfere with the testing process.

What Should Students Expect on Test Day?

Tests for kindergarteners will generally be given in a group or individual setting based on the age of the student, the particular test used, and the resources/preferences of the school. Typically, the examiner will read the directions to the examinee or small group of examinees. If the test is administered individually, the examiner may bubble in the choices on behalf of the student. If the exam is administered in a group setting, examinees will typically be responsible for bubbling in their own answers. In some cases, the tests are given online and not with a paper and pencil.

Typically, you will be given specific information on how (and sometimes by whom) the test will be administered. You should contact the school and ask these types of questions if the answers are not provided beforehand.

What Happens After the Test?

The CogAT is a norm-referenced assessment, meaning students are scored based on a comparison with other students of the same age and grade. First, a raw score is calculated based on the total number of questions answered correctly. The raw score is then used to calculate three types of scores.

1. The **STANDARD AGE SCORE (SAS)** compares a student with other students of the same age. A score of 100 represents average cognitive development. A score higher than 116 (accounting for the standard deviation) suggests a student might have greater cognitive development than others of the same age.

2. The **NATIONAL PERCENTILE RANK (NPR)** compares a student to his/her peers. For example, a 75 percentile rank shows that a student scored better than 75 percent of test takers of the same age and grade.

3. A **STANINE (STANDARD NINE)** is a number between 1 and 9, with 1 indicating lowest performance and 9 indicating highest performance.

The OLSAT is also a norm-referenced assessment. First, a raw score of the total number of items answered correctly is calculated. This is then converted into a **SCHOOL ABILITY INDEX (SAI)**. The SAI is a number up to 150 generated by comparing students to other test takers of the same age and grade. The average score is 100, and the standard deviation is 16. Students who score higher than 116 are identified as having more advanced cognitive development. Like the CogAT, the OLSAT also expresses scores in a percentile rank that compares a student's score with those of other test takers of the same age and grade.

The NNAT is a norm-referenced assessment scored identically to the OLSAT. The converted raw score is referred to as the **NAGLIERI ABILITY INDEX (NAI)** rather than the SAI.

Every school will use test scores differently. Teachers will use your child's test scores, along with other school-specific criteria, to determine if your child should be placed in a gifted education program.

Part I

Verbal Skills

Skills Tested: listening comprehension, vocabulary, logical reasoning

Foundational Knowledge: English language skills

<u>**Directions:**</u> **Choose the picture that BEST answers the question. (Each question will have specific directions that should be read to the student.)**

Diana thought she had lost her backpack, but she found it under the table. Which picture shows Diana's backpack?

Answer Explanation

Diana lost her backpack, but she found it.
WHERE did she find it?
She found it **UNDER** the table.
This picture shows the backpack **UNDER THE TABLE**.

Teaching Tips

→ Many of these questions will require the student to be familiar with the meaning of common prepositions (e.g., *between, near, under, next to, on*).

→ Encourage your student to pay careful attention to negative constructions (such as NOT) in questions.

→ Avoid using special inflection to key cue words as you read the prompts to your student. The examiner will not do this during the exam.

1. Hillary's mother said she had to eat breakfast, brush her teeth, and put on her shoes before she could go outside and swing. Hillary has already eaten breakfast and brushed her teeth. Which of these pictures shows what Hillary still has left to do before she goes outside to swing?

2. Which picture shows an animal that people ride?

3. Which one of these pictures shows a star between a heart and an arrow?

4. Which picture shows this: Rob is eating ice cream. He is wearing shorts and a cowboy hat.

5. Which picture shows a bird in a tree, a cow eating grass, and a horse galloping while the sun is shining?

6. Which picture shows a person who is neither driving a car nor eating?

7. Which picture shows a child in a red shirt and a child in a blue shirt who are playing together?

8. Which picture shows something you would NOT find in a school?

9. Ada took her glasses, a watch, and a comb out of her purse. Which picture shows Ada's purse?

10. On Max's desk, the crayon is between the book and the paper. Which picture shows Max's desk?

11. Which picture shows something a musician would use?

12. Which person delivers letters?

13. Which picture shows this: A lamp is on the table, a purse is on a chair, and a hat is on the floor?

14. Which picture shows something you would find BOTH at the beach AND at a swimming pool?

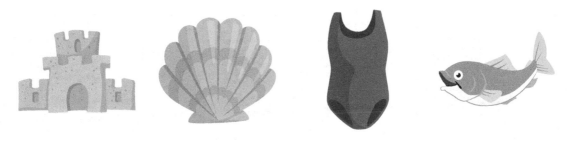

15. Which picture has a banana at the beginning, an apple in the middle, and grapes at the end?

16. Which picture shows something you would NOT use with a ball?

17. Which picture shows something that is NOT worn when it is cold outside?

18. Alice has a cat, a goldfish, a horse, and a puppy. Which picture shows Alice's pets?

19. Which picture shows a plate between a knife and a fork?

20. Which picture shows this: Jeff is playing the piano. He is wearing a hat. His mom is watching.

21. Which picture shows something that CANNOT fly?

22. Rick has chores to do before he can go swimming. He must take out the trash, feed the dog, and sweep the floor. Rick has already taken out the trash and fed the dog. What does he have left to do before he can go swimming?

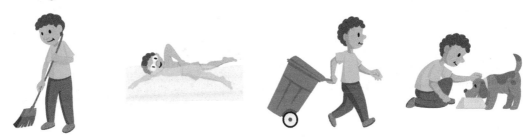

23. Which picture shows an umbrella with a rabbit and a frog underneath it?

24. Which picture shows Veronica walking on a balance beam?

25. Which shows something that a baby would NOT use?

Completing the Sentence

1.

2.

3.

4.

5.

6.

7.

8.

9.

10.

11.

12.

13.

14.

15.

16.

Completing the Sentence (continued)

17.

18.

19.

20.

21.

22.

23.

24.

25.

<u>**Directions:**</u> **Which picture goes BEST in the box with the question mark?**

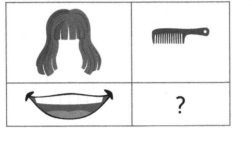

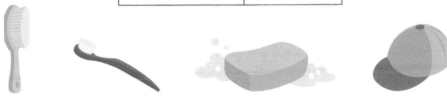

Answer Explanation

Explain to your student that a <u>comb</u> is used to BRUSH <u>hair</u> and a <u>toothbrush</u> is used to BRUSH <u>teeth</u>.

Teaching Tips

→ Common sources of images for picture analogies include sports, farms, animals, school supplies, and household objects.

→ A process of elimination, or "best guess," strategy can be helpful if your student becomes stuck. In the sample question, for example, you can encourage your student to see that "toothbrush" is the best guess because it is the only answer item that has any relationship to teeth.

→ A common mistake is for students to use the same relationship in multiple back-to-back items. For example, if one question focuses on objects used in a school, the student may choose a school-related item as the answer to the next question. You should reinforce that the relationship in each question is different.

1.

2.

3.

 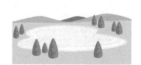 

4.

5.

6.

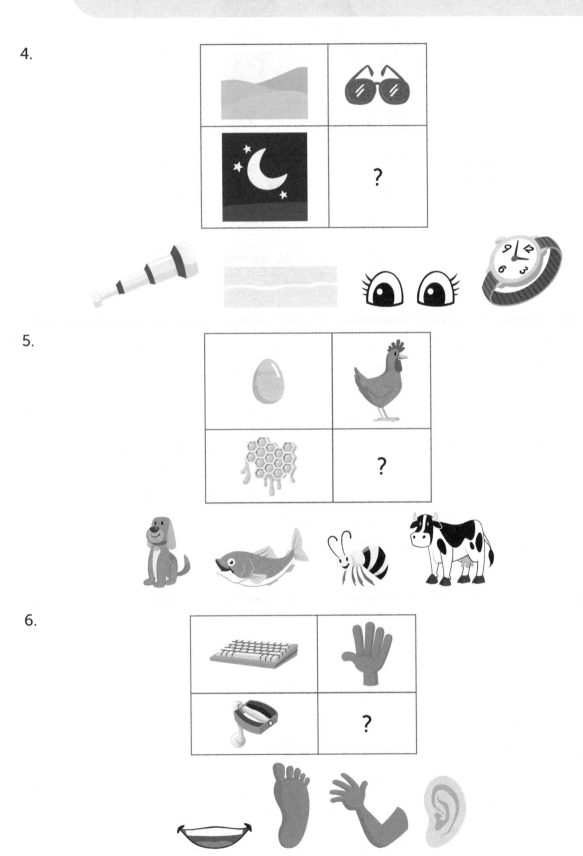

7.

8.

9.

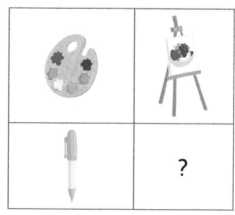

10.

11.

12.

13.

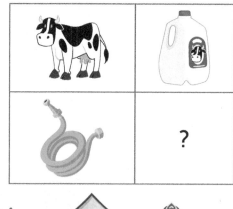

| | |
| | **?** |

14.

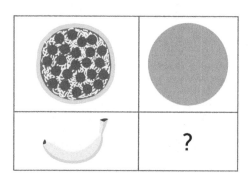

| | |
| banana | **?** |

15.

| tadpole |  |
| caterpillar | **?** |

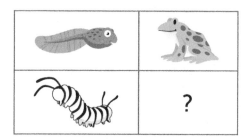

Picture Analogies

1.  A brick is part of a house, and a tire is part of a car.

2. A bird eats a worm, and a human eats a hamburger.

3. A deer lives in a forest, and a fish lives in a lake.

4. Sunglasses are used during the day, and a telescope is used at night.

5. An egg is made by a chicken, and a honeycomb is made by a bee.

6. A hand is used to operate a keyboard, and a foot is used to operate a pedal on a bicycle.

7. A horse is used by a cowboy, and a firetruck is used by a firefighter.

8. Spaghetti is eaten with a fork, and soup is eaten with a spoon.

9. Paint is used to create a painting, and a pen is used to create a letter.

10. When there is snow, people wear a coat, and when there is sun, people wear shorts.

11. Milk is eaten with cereal, and ketchup is eaten with french fries.

12. A gate is the entry to a pasture, and a door is the entry to a house.

13. A cow produces milk, and a hose produces water.

14. A pizza is a circular shape, and a banana is a crescent shape.

15. A tadpole becomes a frog, and a caterpillar becomes a butterfly.

Chapter 3

Comparing Pictures (Similarities)

Skills Tested:
making logical connections

Foundational Knowledge:
comparative terms

<u>Directions:</u> **Look at the pictures. One of the pictures belongs with the others because it is similar in some way. Which picture belongs with the others?**

Question			
Answers			

Answer Explanation

A cell phone, like a radio, a television, and a microwave, is an electronic device. Point to each of the four similar items as you say, "Radio, television, microwave, cell phone. These are all types of electronic devices."

Mime or draw an X over the house and the ear as you say, "House and ear are NOT types of electronic devices."

Teaching Tips

→ A common mistake is to make an association between only two of the objects (e.g., between a radio and an ear) versus considering the shared relationship between all the objects. Encourage your student to point to each of the first three objects in the top row to ensure that they have thoroughly studied the question.

→ While practicing, your student might encounter an image that is simply unfamiliar. When this happens, talk about the image and show your student the corresponding real-life object, if possible. Sometimes, the way a certain object is drawn may differ from the way your student might expect, and it is helpful to show the connection between images and tangible objects.

1.			
Question			
Answers			

2.			
Question			
Answers			

3.			
Question			
Answers			

4.			
Question			
Answers			

5.

Question			
Answers			

6.

Question			
Answers			

7.

Question			Dearest Rachel, This is a letter that children should hopefully recognize. Love, Mom
Answers			

8.

Question			
Answers	STOP		

9.			
Question			
Answers			

10.			
Question			
Answers			

11.			
Question			
Answers			

12.			
Question			
Answers			

13.

Question			
Answers			

14.

Question			
Answers			

15.

Question			
Answers			

16.

Question			
Answers			

Comparing Pictures (Similarities)

1. The crayon, pencil, marker, and **pen** are all writing instruments.

2. The icicles, frozen pond, snowflakes, and **snowman** are all related to cold weather.

3. The hand, ear, foot, and **arm** are all body parts.

4. The house, doghouse, bird's nest, and **fish tank** are all places where something lives.

5. The apple, orange, grapes, and **banana** are all fruit.

6. The baby, chick, puppy, and **kitten** are all baby animals.

7. The book, newspaper, letter, and **magazine** are all things that can be read.

8. The bicycle, train, car, and **plane** are all types of transportation.

9. The desk, couch, table, and **chair** are all pieces of furniture.

10. The baseball hat, cowboy hat, fireman's hat, and **princess hat** are all types of hats.

11. The elephant, monkey, zebra, and **lion** are all animals.

12. The can, bottle, box, and **purse** are all containers used to hold things.

13. The pliers, hammer, screwdriver, and **wrench** are all tools.

14. The tree, flower, bush, and **grass** are all plants.

15. The hockey stick, tennis racket, cricket mallet, and **baseball bat** are all used to hit balls.

16. The cupcake, ice cream, chocolate, and **doughnut** are all sweet foods.

Chapter 4

Comparing Pictures (Differences)

Skills Tested:
making logical connections

Foundational Knowledge:
comparative terms

Directions: Look at the pictures. One of the pictures doesn't belong with the others because it is different in some way. Which picture doesn't belong?

Answer Explanation

A flower is not something associated with fishing. Say the category or shared attribute first: "All pictures are part of fishing."

Next, point to each picture as you say, "A fishing pole. A worm. A fish. A net."

Finally, point to the flower and say, "A flower is NOT part of fishing."

Teaching Tips

→ If your student answers incorrectly, cover up the item that does not belong and then ask a leading question, like "Where do these animals live?" or "What do these objects do?" Once the similar relationship is established, uncover the correct answer and reinforce: "This animal does NOT live in..." or "This object does NOT...."

→ Your student might find it easier to draw an X with their finger or a pencil over the object that does not belong to reinforce the concept of difference. However, you still want to make sure your student has plenty of practice filling in the bubble for the correct answer, so always make this the final step in solving any problem.

1.

2.

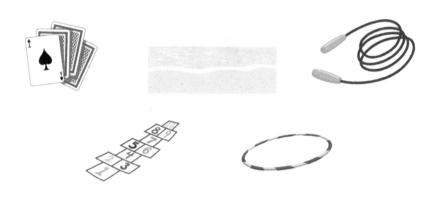

3.

4.

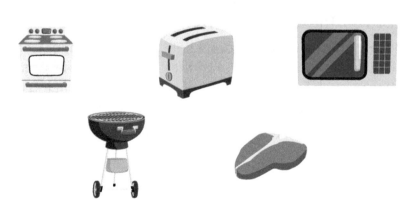

5.

6.

7.

8.

9.

10.

11.

12.

13.

14.

15.

Comparing Pictures (Differences)

1. A tree does not make noise.

2. A beach is not a game.

3. A police officer is not imaginary.

4. A steak is not a device that is used to cook something.

5. A pencil is not a vegetable.

6. A snake does not produce light.

7. An ear is not a weapon.

8. A bed is not a part of a car.

9. A snail does not move quickly.

10. A boat does not have wheels.

11. Cereal is not a dairy product.

12. Pizza is not cold.

13. A sandwich is not round.

14. A laundry basket is not used to track time.

15.  A camel is not something one would find at the beach.

Chapter 5

Picture Series

Skills Tested:
making logical connections, pattern recognition, understanding sequence of events

Foundational Knowledge:
chronological order

Directions: Look at the pictures in the boxes and see how they go together in a certain way. Look at the next row of pictures. Which picture belongs next in the series of questions?

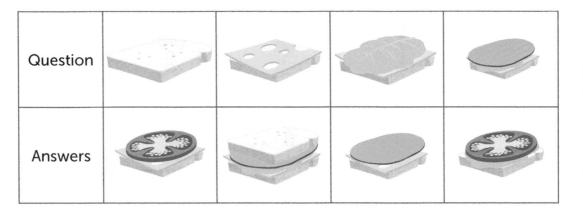

Answer Explanation

Say, "The pictures show someone making a sandwich."

Point to each step in the process as you explain: "First, they have one piece of bread. Then they add cheese. Then they add lettuce. Then they add ham."

Point to the correct answer and say, "Next, they add the top piece of bread to finish the sandwich."

Teaching Tips

→ Focus your student's attention on "finishing" the story or sequence by determining what happens NEXT. This can be modeled by pointing to each item in the series and saying, "First, next, then, after, finally...." or "First, second, third, fourth, fifth...."

→ Remind your student that processes are not always additive but may involve removing parts or pieces.

→ Incorrect answer choices may be images of something that occurred BEFORE the series of events. Remind your student that the answer will always be something that happens AFTER.

1.

Question				
Answers				

2.

Question				
Answers				

3.

Question				
Answers				

4.

Question				
Answers				

5.

Question				
Answers				

6.

Question				
Answers				

7.

Question				
Answers				

8.

Question				
Answers				

9.				
Question				
Answers				

10.				
Question				
Answers				

11.				
Question				
Answers				

12.				
Question				
Answers				

13.

Question				
Answers				

14.

Question				
Answers				

15.

Question				
Answers				

Picture Series

1. The number of tennis rackets and balls is decreasing by one in each picture. The next picture will have **one racket** and **one ball**.

2. The balloon is filled with more air in each picture. The next picture will show the **balloon popping**.

3. The pizza is losing one slice in each picture. The next picture will have **four slices removed** (half a pie).

4. The number of petals on the flower is increasing by one in each picture. The next picture will have **six petals**.

5. The pictures show a man baking cookies. The next picture will show the man **eating the cookies**.

6. The pictures show a chicken hatching from an egg and growing. The next picture will show the **full-grown chicken**.

7. The number of fingers held up is increasing by one in each picture. The next picture will show **four fingers** being held up.

8. The pictures show a plant growing from a seed in a pot. The next picture will show the **flowering plant** in the pot.

9. The pictures show two children building a tall tower from blocks. The next picture will show the **tower falling over**.

10. The pictures show one eye that is opening. The next picture will show **one fully open eye.**

11. The pictures show a child going to bed and waking up in the morning. The next picture will show the boy **brushing his teeth** in the morning.

12. The pictures show lines being drawn to make a stick figure. The next picture will be the **complete stick figure**.

13. The pictures show a table being set. The final picture will show the full table setting with a **plate, fork, spoon, and knife**.

14. The pictures show a child waking up, eating breakfast, and getting on the bus to school. The next picture will show the **child in school**.

15. The bowl is losing one orange in each picture. The next picture will show a **bowl with two oranges**.

Part II

Math Skills

Chapter 6

Number Analogies

Skills Tested: graphic literacy, counting, addition (counting up), subtraction (counting down)

Foundational Knowledge: basic counting skills, analogies

Directions: Which figure goes best in the box with the question mark?

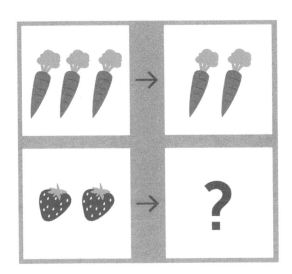

Answer Explanation

First, count the carrots in the left box.

Next, count the carrots in the right box.

What happened to the carrots?

One carrot **went away** or was **taken away.**

The box on the left has two strawberries. We need to take one strawberry away.

One strawberry goes in the box.

Teaching Tips

→ Start by having your student identify the relationship in the top boxes. Is the number of objects going up or down? How many objects have been added or taken away?

→ These questions require students to count up (add) or count down (subtract), but they don't have to understand mathematical symbols (+, −, =).

→ Avoid creating arithmetic equations (e.g., 3 − 1 = 2) unless your student is already very familiar with such equations.

1.

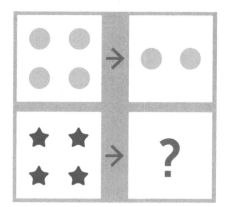

2.

3.

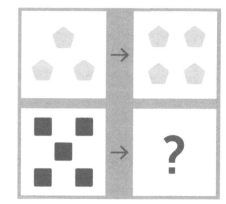

4.

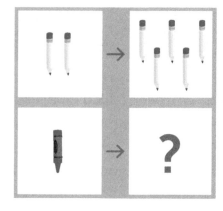

5.

6.

7.

8.

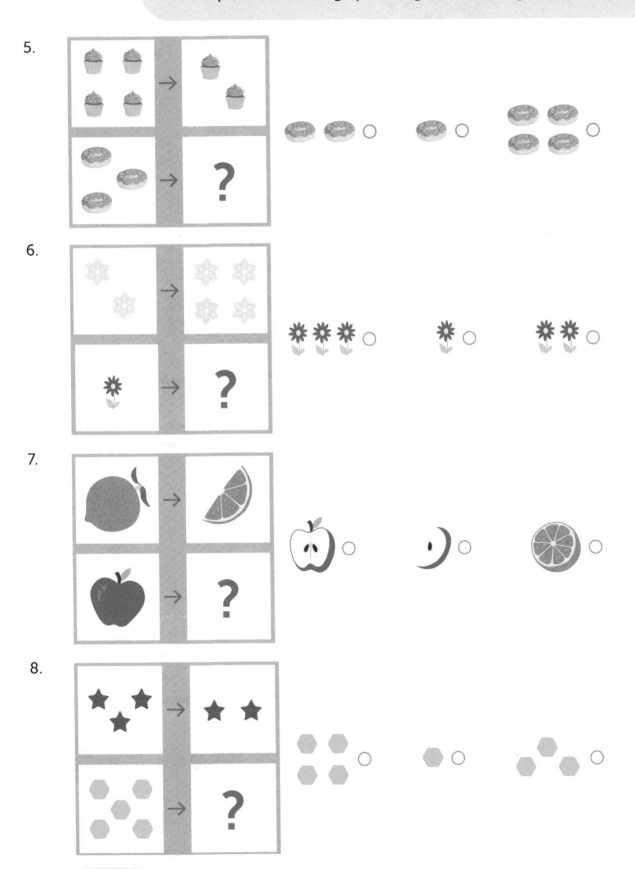

9.

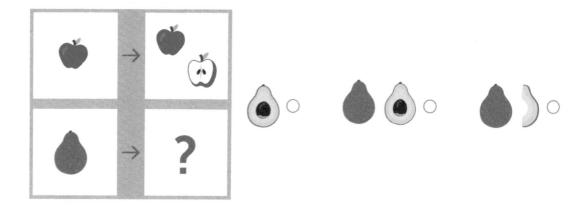

10.

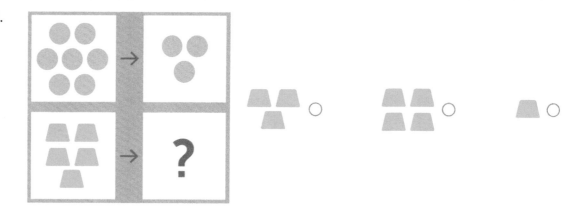

11.

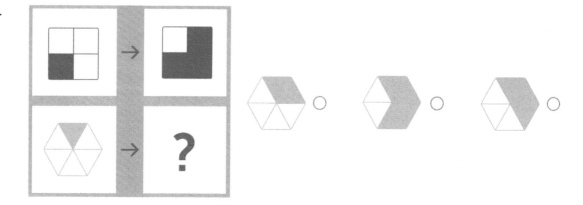

12.

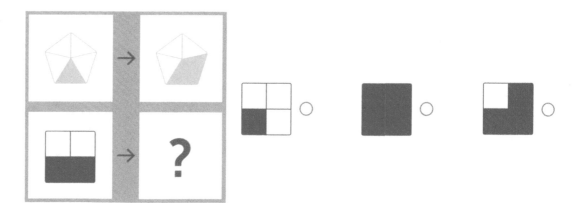

13.

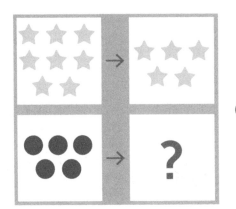

● ● ● ○   ● ● ○   ● ○

14.

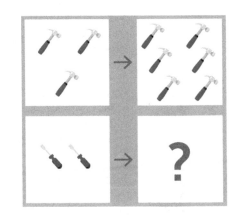

15.

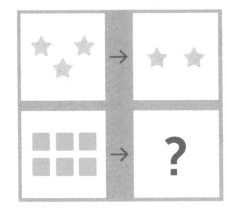

Number Analogies

1.

Two circles have been taken away, so two stars should be taken away: 4 − 2 = 2.

2.

The orange has been cut in half, so the tomato should be cut in half.

3.

One pentagon has been added, so one square should be added: 5 + 1 = 6.

4.

Three pencils have been added, so three crayons should be added: 1 + 3 = 4.

5.

Two cupcakes have been taken away, so two donuts should be taken away: 3 − 2 = 1.

6.

Two snowflakes have been added, so two flowers should be added: 1 + 2 = 3.

7.

Three-quarters of the orange has been taken away, so three-quarters of the apple should be taken away.

8.

One star has been taken away, so one hexagon should be taken away: 5 − 1 = 4.

9.

One-fifth of the pentagon has been filled in, so one-fourth of the square should be filled in.

10.

Half of an apple has been added, so half of an avocado should be added.

11.

Four circles have been removed, so four trapezoids should be removed: 5 − 4 = 1.

12.

Two-fourths of the square have been filled, so two-sixths of the pentagon should be filled.

13.

Three stars have been taken away, so three circles should be taken away: 5 − 3 = 2.

14.

Three hammers have been added, so three screwdrivers should be added: 2 + 3 = 5.

15.

One star has been taken away, so one square should be taken away: 6 − 1 = 5.

Chapter 7

Number Puzzles

Skills Tested:
counting, understanding of equivalence/equality

Foundational Knowledge:
basic counting skills, graphic literacy

Directions: Which choice best completes the picture?

Answer Explanation

First, count the tomatoes in the top train car.

Next, count the tomatoes in the train car next to the question mark.

How many more tomatoes do we need to make three?

We have two tomatoes. We need one more tomato to make three.

Teaching Tips

→ Method one: test each answer option for equivalency. First, have your student count the objects in the top picture. Next, have them count the objects in the car next to the question mark. Lastly, have them count up from that value for each answer choice.
one, two . . . three (first option)
one, two . . . three, four (second option)
one, two . . . three, four, five (third option)

→ Method two: treat the question as a subtraction problem. First, have the student count the quantity in the top picture. Then have the student look at the quantity in the second row and ask, "How many are missing?" The correct answer corresponds to the number of tomatoes that is missing.

→ Method three: circle the "extra quantity" in the top row so that the student can visually identify the answer choice.

1.

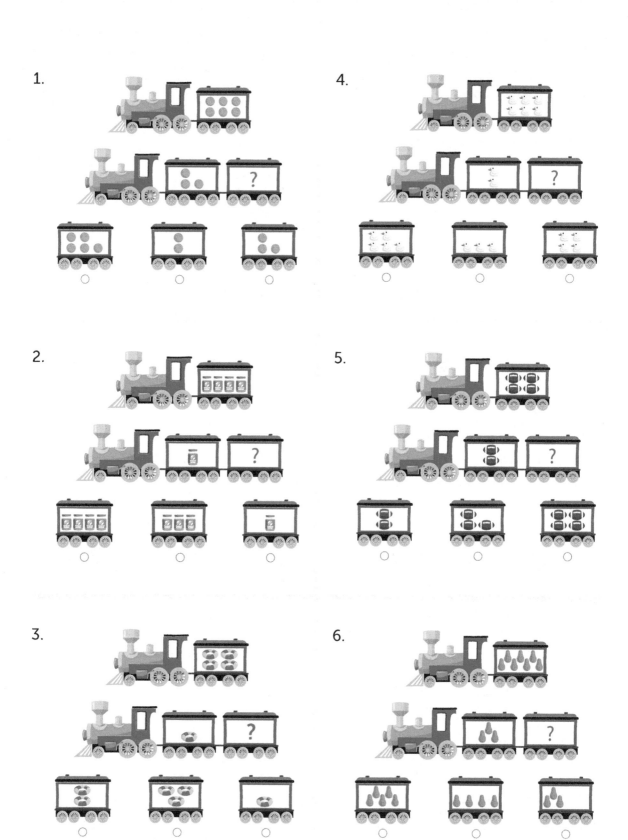

2.

3.

4.

5.

6.

7.

10.

8.

11.

9.

12.

13.

14.

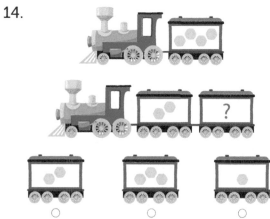

15.

Number Puzzles

1.  6 − 3 = 3

2.  4 − 1 = 3

3.  4 − 1 = 3

4.  6 − 2 = 4

5.  4 − 2 = 2

6.  7 − 3 = 4

7.  8 − 5 = 3

8. 6 − 4 = 2

9.  5 − 4 = 1

10.  7 − 2 = 5

11.  8 − 5 = 3

12.  5 − 4 = 1

13. 8 − 5 = 3

14. 4 − 2 = 2

15. 10 − 4 = 6

Directions: Which choice completes the pattern?

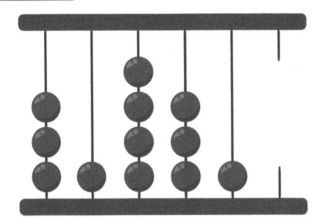 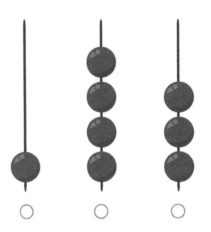

Answer Explanation

Let's find the pattern. Three, one, four, three, one, _____.

(Draw a vertical line to show where the pattern starts to repeat.)

The pattern on the left side of the line is three, one, four.

Complete the pattern on the right side of the line: three, one, . . . four.

Teaching Tips

→ Patterns can be of any type, and they may or may not repeat. (Some patterns may simply ascend or descend.)

→ Students can confirm or double-check their answer by restating the pattern from the beginning and including their answer choice at the end.

→ It can save time if your student can instantly recognize quantities without counting each bead, but it's not necessary to be successful on these problems.

1.

2.

3.

4.

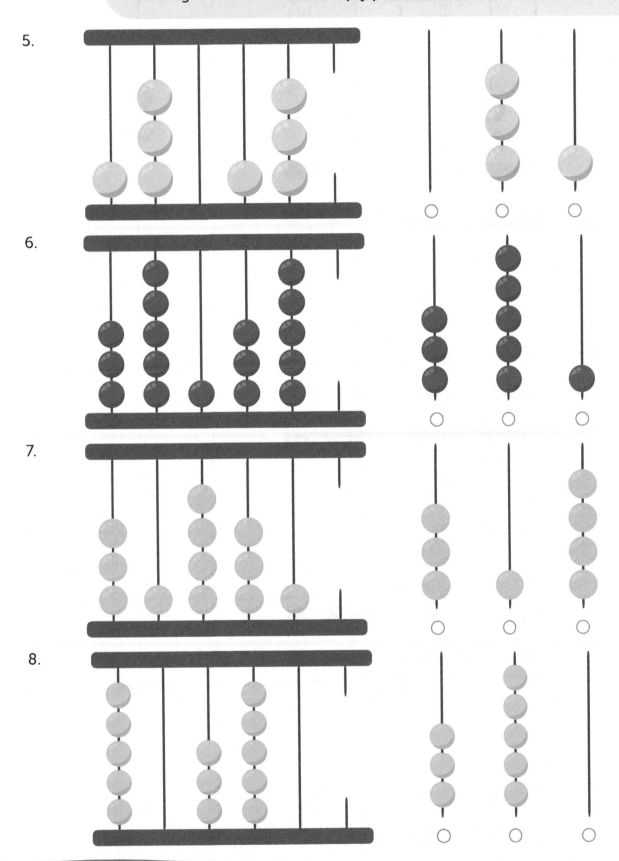

5.

6.

7.

8.

9.

10.

11.

12.

56

13.

14.

15.

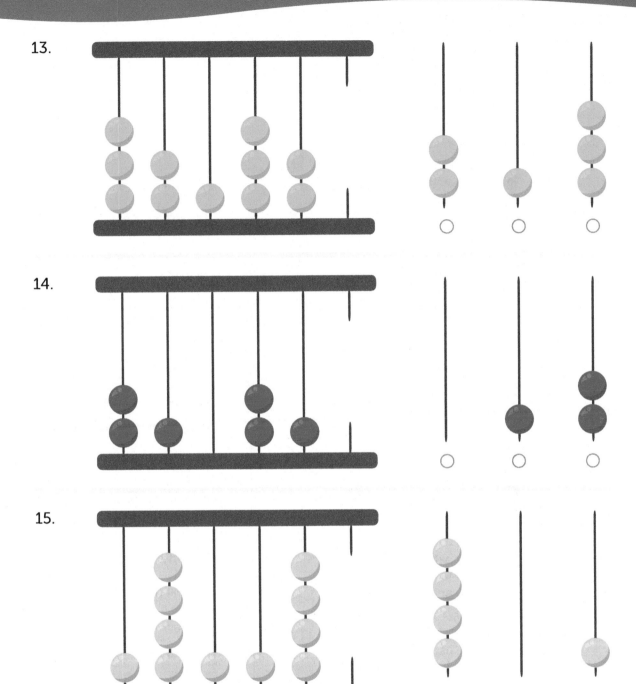

Number Series

1.
The pattern is
1, 2, 3, ...
The next number is 3.

2.
The pattern is
0, 1, 2, 0, ...
The next number is 2.

3.
The pattern is
3, 0, 2, ...
The next number is 2.

4.
The pattern is
1, 2, 4, ...
The next number is 4.

5.
The pattern is
1, 3, 0, ...
The next number is 0.

6.
The pattern is
3, 5, 1, ...
The next number is 1.

7.
The pattern is
3, 1, 4, ...
The next number is 4.

8.
The pattern is
5, 0, 3, ...
The next number is 3.

9.
The pattern is
0, 2, 1, ...
The next number is 1.

10.
The pattern is
2, 0, 1, ...
The next number is 1.

11.
The pattern is
1, 5, 4, ...
The next number is 4.

12.
The pattern is
3, 1, 0, ...
The next number is 0.

13.
The pattern is
3, 2, 1, ...
The next number is 1.

14.
The pattern is
2, 1, 0, ...
The next number is 0.

15.
The pattern is
1, 4, 1, ...
The next number is 1.

Chapter 9

Arithmetic Reasoning

Directions: Choose the picture that BEST answers the question. (Each question will have specific directions that should be read to the student.)

The picture at the beginning shows a number of pencils. If three children take one pencil each, how many pencils would be left?

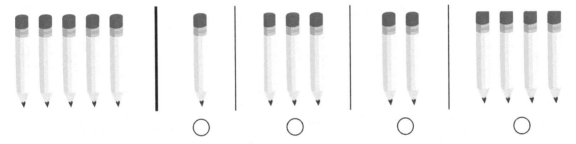

Answer Explanation

Point to the first image and count: "One, two, three, four, five pencils."

Next, say: "Three children each take away one pencil," and draw a line through "1, 2, 3 pencils" as you count aloud.

Say: "How many pencils are left?"

Count: "One, two pencils are left" as you point to the two remaining pencils.

Teaching Tips

→ These items may contain higher-level math concepts like division and multiplication, but you should avoid the temptation to use equations or mathematical symbols (like ÷ or ×). An understanding of these symbols is NOT necessary to be successful with these item types.

→ Understanding the concepts of halving or doubling can be very useful for some of these item types. Practice halving and doubling within base 10 (numbers that do not exceed ten when doubled) with tangible objects.

→ It can be challenging for young students to remember or to "hold" numbers in their head when they hear them. If your student struggles with this, encourage them to begin solving the problem immediately in the first image. For example, if they hear that two children each get an item, they might immediately circle two of the items in the first box.

1. The picture at the beginning of the row shows Hanna's books. Zoey has twice as many books as Hanna. How many books does Zoey have?

○ ○ ○ ○

2. The picture at the beginning shows how many dogs Mark's family already has. If Mark's family gets two more dogs, how many dogs will the family have?

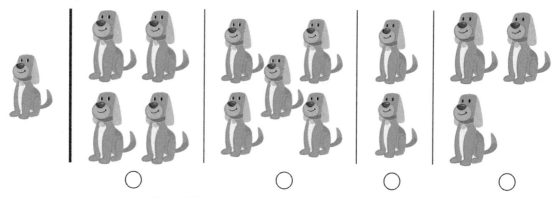
○ ○ ○ ○

3. The picture at the beginning of the row shows how many fish Alex saw at the aquarium on Friday. If Alex saw an equal number of fish at the aquarium on Saturday, how many fish did Alex see on Saturday?

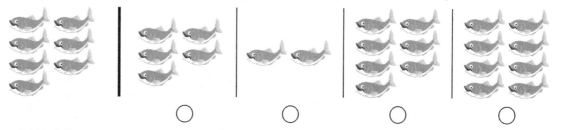
○ ○ ○ ○

4. The picture at the beginning shows a number of seashells. If two children each take two seashells, how many seashells will be left?

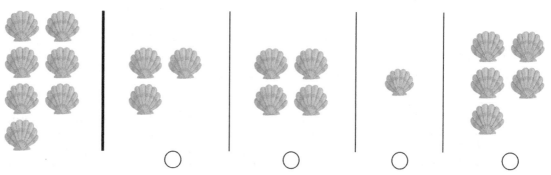
○ ○ ○ ○

5. The picture in the beginning shows how many pumpkins the teacher has. If the teacher gives six students one pumpkin each, how many pumpkins will be left?

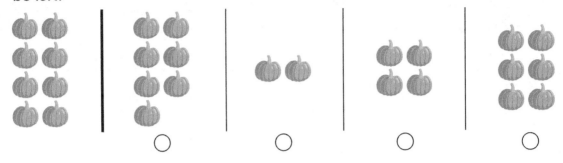

○   ○   ○   ○

6. The picture at the beginning of the row shows how many pairs of scissors Hector has. if Hector gives his friend Tim two pair of scissors, how many pairs of scissors will Hector have left?

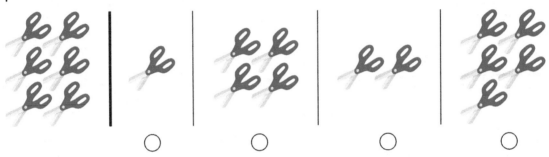

○   ○   ○   ○

7. The picture at the beginning shows a number of birds. If half of the birds fly away, how many birds will be left?

○   ○   ○   ○

8. The box at the beginning of the row shows a number of bananas. If two children take two bananas each, how many bananas will be left?

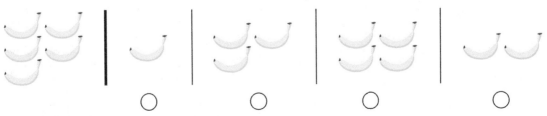

○   ○   ○   ○

9. The picture at the beginning of the row shows a number of cars. If half of the cars are sold, how many cars would be left?

⃝   ⃝   ⃝   ⃝

10. The picture at the beginning shows a number of crayons. If all eight students in the class take one crayon, how many crayons would be left?

⃝   ⃝   ⃝   ⃝

11. The first picture shows how many horses live on Dan's farm. If Tom's farm has three more horses than Dan's, how many horses live on Tom's farm?

⃝   ⃝   ⃝   ⃝

12. The first picture shows how many cupcakes there are. If two children each get one cupcake, how many cupcakes will be left?

⃝   ⃝   ⃝   ⃝

13. The box at the beginning shows how many blocks are on the shelf. Virginia and Lacy each take an equal number of blocks, and no blocks are left on the shelf. How many blocks did each girl take?

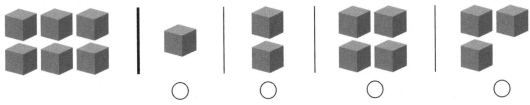

        ◯   ◯   ◯   ◯

14. The first picture shows how many stars Andre has. If Jordan has four more stars than Andre, how many stars does Jordan have?

        ◯   ◯   ◯   ◯

15. The box at the beginning shows the number of cookies Maya has. If David has three times as many cookies as Maya, how many cookies does David have?

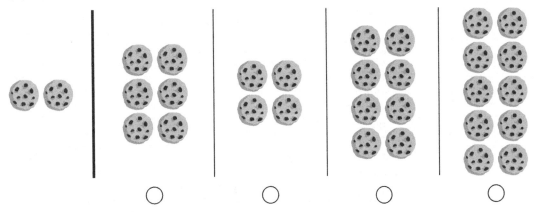

        ◯   ◯   ◯   ◯

Arithmetic Reasoning

1. Hanna has four books. If Zoey has twice as many books, she has 4 × 2 = **8** books.

2. Mark's family has one dog. If they get two more dogs, they will have 2 + 1 = **3** dogs.

3. Alex saw seven fish on Friday. If she saw the same number on Saturday, then she saw **7** fish.

4. There are seven seashells. If two children each take two shells, there will be 7 − (2 × 2) = **3** shells left.

5. The teacher has eight pumpkins. If the teacher gives six students one pumpkin each, she will have 8 − 6 = **2** pumpkins left.

6. Hector has six pairs of scissors. If he gives away two pairs of scissors, he will have 6 − 2 = **4** pairs of scissors left.

7. There are four birds. If half the birds fly away, there will be 4 ÷ 2 = **2** birds left.

8. There are five bananas. If two children each take two bananas, there will be 5 − (2 × 2) = **1** banana left.

9. There are six cars. If half the cars are sold, there will be 6 ÷ 2 = **3** cars left.

10. There are 10 crayons. If eight students each take one crayon, there will be 10 − 8 = **2** crayons left.

11. Dan's farm has five horses. If Tom's farm has three more horses, then Tom's farm has 5 + 3 = **8** horses.

12. There are three cupcakes. If two children each take one cupcake, there will be 3 − 2 = **1** cupcake left.

13. There are six blocks on the shelf. If Virginia and Lacy each take an equal number of blocks and there are no blocks left, each girl will have taken 6 ÷ 2 = **3** blocks.

14. Andre has six stars. If Jordan has four more stars than Andre, then Jordan has 6 + 4 = **10** stars.

15. Maya has two cookies. If David has three times as many cookies as Maya, then David has 2 × 3 = **6** cookies.

Part III

Spatial Skills

Chapter 10

Comparing Figures (Finding Similarities)

Skills Tested: identifying details, making logical connections

Foundational Knowledge: basic shapes, colors, comparative terms

Directions: The pictures on the top row show three objects that belong together in a certain way. Choose the picture from the bottom row that goes with the three objects on top.

○   ○   ○

Answer Explanation

What is the **same** about all of these shapes?

The shapes in the top row have another shape inside them.

The triangle is the **same**. It has two shapes like the other shapes.

Teaching Tips

→ Your student may benefit from a ritualized method for answering these item types. For example, have your student point to each of the three objects and then point to each of the answer options.

→ This method may also include verbal reinforcement, such as stating the shared traits of the shape while pointing at each one.

1.

○   ○   ○

4.

○   ○   ○

2.

○   ○   ○

5.

○   ○   ○

3.

○   ○   ○

6.

○   ○   ○

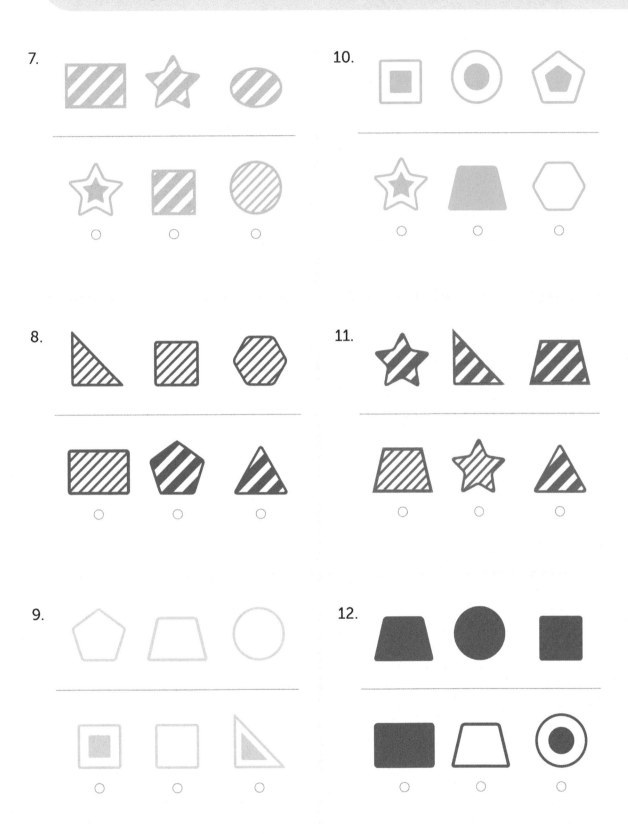

7.

8.

9.

10.

11.

12.

13.

○   ○   ○

14

○   ○   ○

15.

○   ○   ○

Comparing Figures (Finding Similarities)

1. All the shapes are filled with thin stripes.

2. All the shapes have a smaller shape inside.

3. All the shapes are empty.

4. All the shapes are filled with thick stripes.

5. All the shapes are hexagons.

6. All the shapes are solid.

7. All the shapes are filled with thick stripes.

8. All the shapes are filled with thin stripes.

9. All the shapes are empty.

10. All the shapes have a smaller shape inside.

11. All the shapes are filled with thick stripes.

12. All the shapes are solid.

13. All the shapes are filled with thin stripes.

14. All the shapes are empty.

15. All the shapes are filled with thick stripes.

Chapter 11

Comparing Figures (Finding Differences)

Skills Tested: identifying details, making logical connections

Foundational Knowledge: basic shapes, colors, comparative terms

Directions: The pictures in the top row show three objects that belong together in a certain way. Choose the picture in the bottom row that does not belong with the three objects on top.

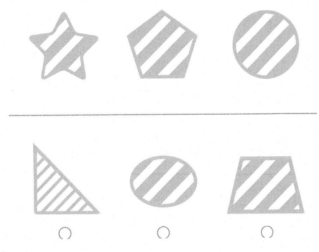

Answer Explanation

What is the same about all of these shapes on top?

They all have big stripes.

Which shape on the bottom is different?

The triangle is different. It has skinny stripes.

Teaching Tips

→ To confirm the answer, have your student cover up the answer they have chosen with one hand, leaving only the similar objects in view. They can then point to the remaining objects while saying same, same, same, same. They can also state what makes the shape the same (e.g., big stripes, big stripes, . . .).

1.

○   ○   ○

2.

○   ○   ○

3.

○   ○   ○

4.

5.

6.
○   ○   ○

7.

○ ○ ○

10.

○ ○ ○

8.

○ ○ ○

11.

○ ○ ○

9.

○ ○ ○

12.

○ ○ ○

13.

○   ○   ○

14

○   ○   ○

15.

○   ○   ○

Comparing Figures (Finding Differences)

1. All the shapes are solid except the hexagon.

2. All the shapes are empty except the star.

3. All the shapes are filled with thin stripes except the pentagon.

4. All the shapes are filled with thick stripes except the equilateral triangle.

5. All the shapes are empty except the pentagon.

6. All the shapes are filled with thin stripes except the circle.

7. All the shapes are stars except the triangle.

8. All the shapes are hexagons except the pentagon.

9. All the shapes are trapezoids except the rectangle.

10. All the shapes are filled with thin stripes except the oval.

11. All the shapes have corners except the circle.

12. All the shapes are rectangles except the square.

13. All the shapes are ovals except the circle.

14. All the shapes are filled with thin stripes except the star.

15. All the shapes have a smaller shape inside except the hexagon

Chapter 12

Figure Analogies

Skills Tested: identifying details, making logical connections, graphic literacy

Foundational Knowledge: basic shapes, colors, analogies

Directions: Which figure goes best in the box with the question mark?

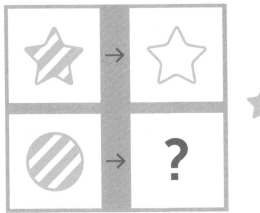

Answer Explanation

What happened to the star? It lost its stripes.

What will happen to the circle? It will lose its stripes.

The striped star becomes the empty star. The striped circle becomes the empty circle.

Teaching Tips

→ Start by showing your student how to read the image like it is text, from left to right and from top to bottom. If your student becomes confused, encourage them to follow the direction of the arrow.

→ Ask your student to identify the relationship between the two objects in the top row. You can ask questions such as *How are the shapes different* or *What changes in the second shape* to encourage them to find the relationship themselves.

→ Once they have found a relationship, ask them to find a shape that has the same relationship in the bottom row.

1.

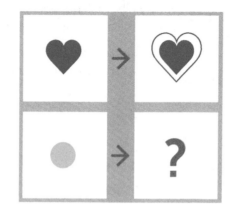

 ○   ○   ○

2.

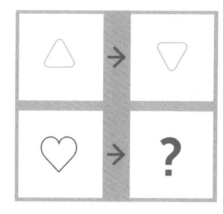

 ○   ○   ○

3.

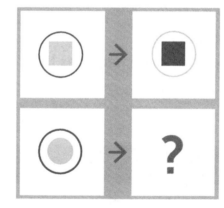

 ○   ○   ○

4.

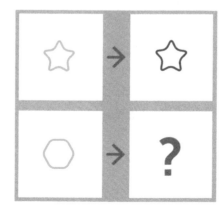

 ○   ○   ○

TEACHING TIP: Use the "I say, we say, you say" method to help reinforce concepts. After you model the way to solve the problem, have the student solve the problem in unison with you. Then, have the student solve the problem on their own.

5.

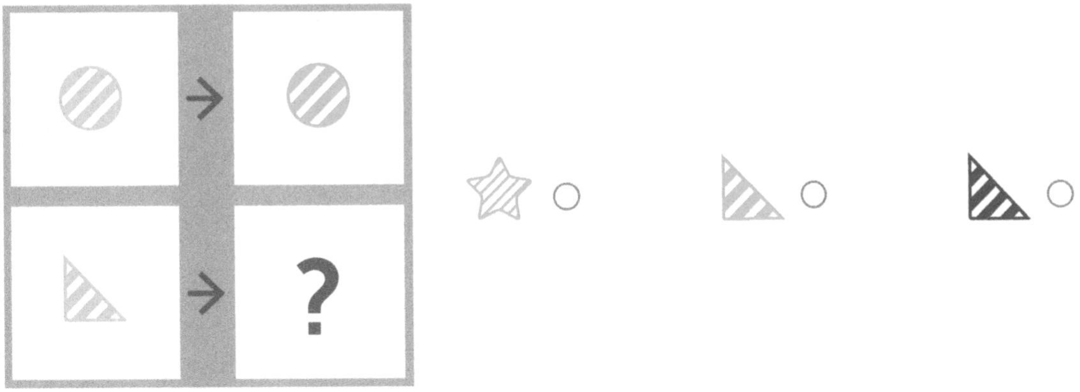

6.

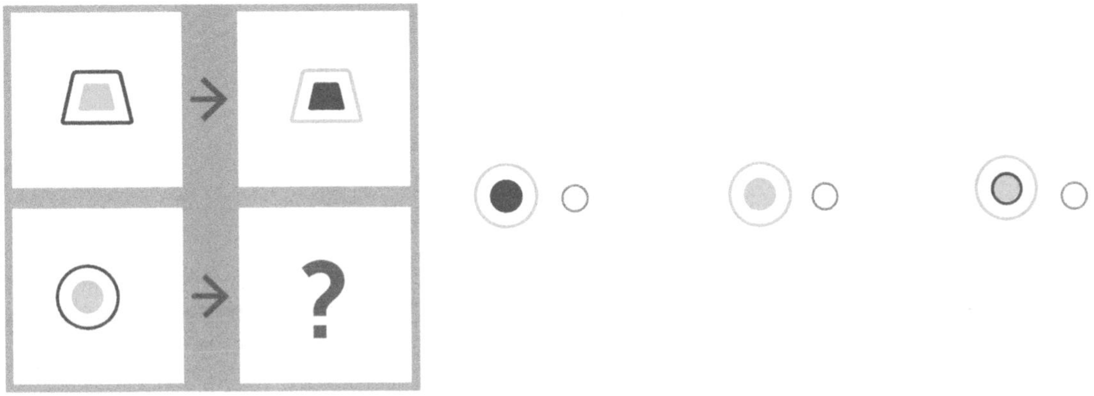

7.

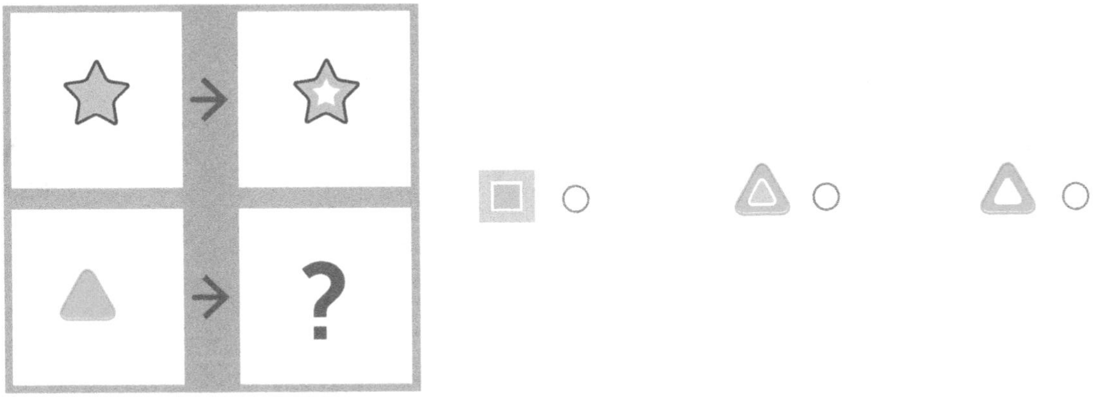

8.

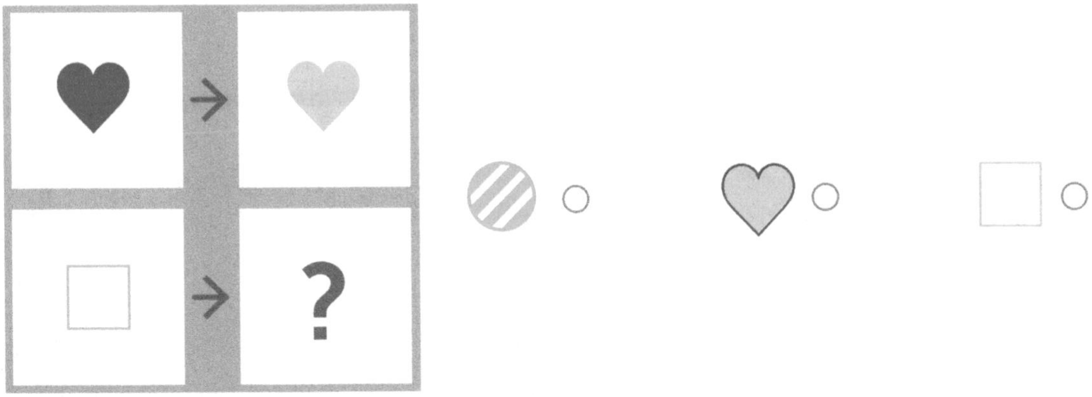

9.

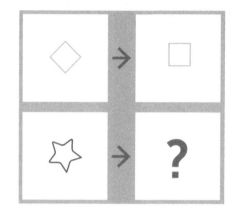

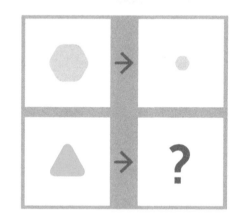

 ○   ○   ○

10.

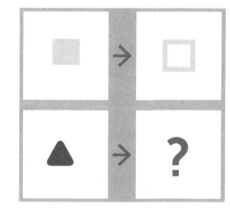

 ○   ○   ○

11.

 ○   ○ ○   ○

12.

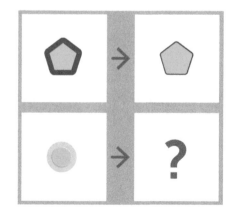

 ○   ○   ○

13.

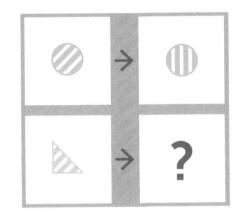 ○   ○    ○

14.

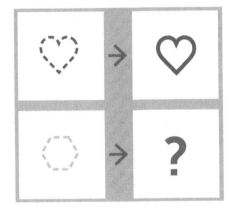 ○   ○   ○

15.

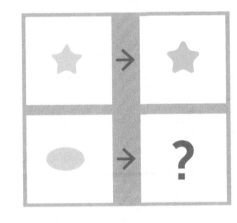 ○   ○   ○

Figure Analogies

1. The shape has a larger outline drawn around it.

2. The shape has turned upside down.

3. The colors in the inner and outer shapes are transposed.

4. The color of the shape changes from green to red.

5. The color of the shape changes from blue to green.

6. The colors in the inner and outer shapes are transposed.

7. A small, white version of the shape is now in the middle

8. The color of the shape changes to blue.

9. The shape rotates 90 degrees.

10. The shape shrinks.

11. The middle of the shape is removed.

12. The outline around the shape is thinner.

13. The shape rotates 270 degrees.

14. The color of the shape changes blue to green.

15. The line around the shape changes from dashed to solid.

Directions: Which shows what the paper will look like when it is unfolded?

Answer Explanation

These white spaces are cuts in the paper. How many cuts are there?

There are three cuts. There is a notch cut in the top of the paper and two slits cut in the bottom (point to the white area in the final image of the question). These cuts match the notches and slits in the answer.

Teaching Tips

→ Help your student understand that the pictures show a process (first, second, third, fourth, and then a final product).

→ Ensure your student can interpret the symbols in the problem.

　→ Arrows show the direction in which the paper is folded.

　→ Dashed lines or solid lines show the area of the unfolded paper.

　→ White areas show cuts or holes in the paper.

→ You can use a real piece of paper to model the steps in the problem, stopping at each step to show your student how each cut looks when then the paper is unfolded.

1.

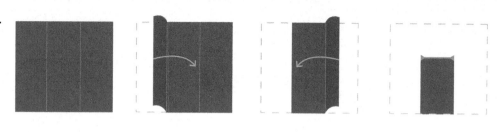

○ ○ ○

2.

○ ○ ○

3.

○ ○ ○

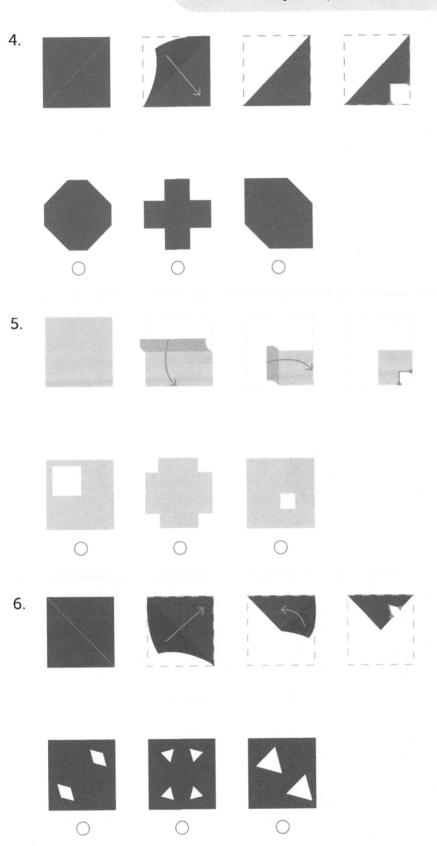

4.

○ ○ ○

5.

○ ○ ○

6.

○ ○ ○

7.

◯ ◯ ◯

8.

◯ ◯ ◯

9.

◯ ◯ ◯

10.

   ○   ○   ○

11.

   ○   ○   ○

12.

   ○   ○   ○

13.

○ ○ ○

14.

○ ○ ○

15.

○ ○ ○

Paper Folding

1.

2.

3.

4.

5.

6.

7.

8.

9.

10.

11.

12.

13.

14.

15.

Chapter 14

Pattern Matrices

Skills Tested: identifying details, making logical connections, graphic literacy skills

Foundational Knowledge: basic shapes, colors, matrices

Directions: Which picture comes next?

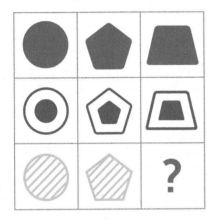

Answer Explanation

Let's identify the pattern across: circle, pentagon, trapezoid.

Let's identify the pattern down: solid, small shape inside, small stripes.

What goes next?

The trapezoid with the small stripes fits both patterns.

Circle, pentagon, trapezoid. (While pointing to third row.)

Solid, small shape, smalls stripes. (While pointing to third column.)

Teaching Tips

→ Have students "read" the problem by looking for the horizontal pattern and then the vertical pattern.

→ Make sure your student knows to look only for horizontal or vertical patterns (not diagonal ones).

→ Encourage students to consider multiple attributes of each object (e.g., shape and color).

1.

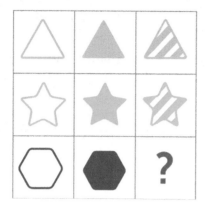

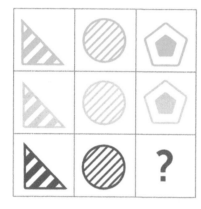

2.

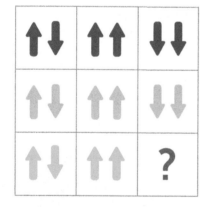

3.

4.

TEACHING TIP: Provide lots of positive reinforcement. These questions are different from the ones most students see in school, and they may take some time to figure out what they're being asked to do.

5.

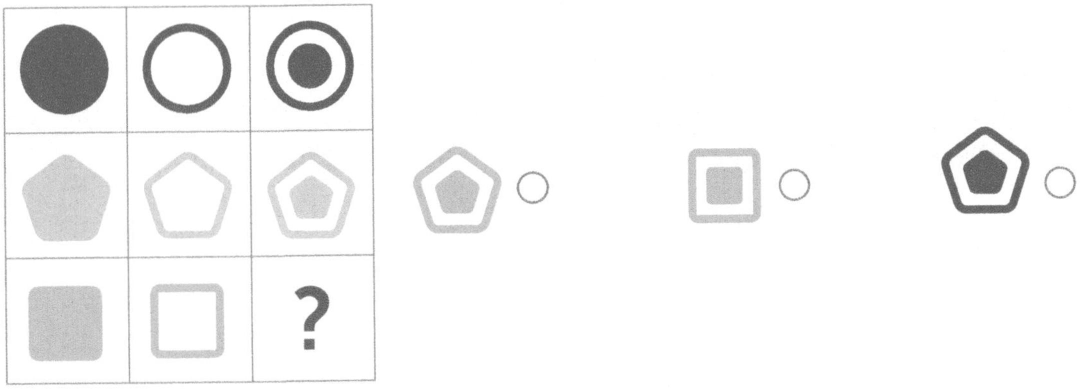

6.

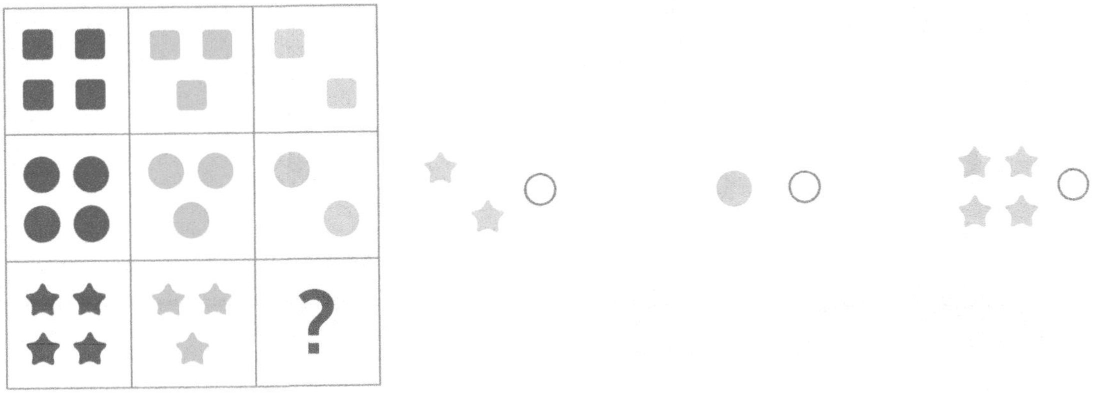

7.

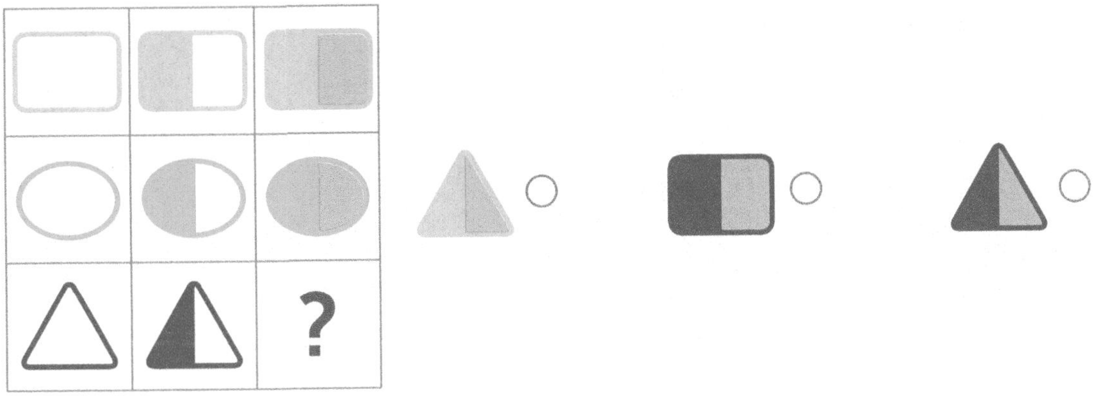

8.

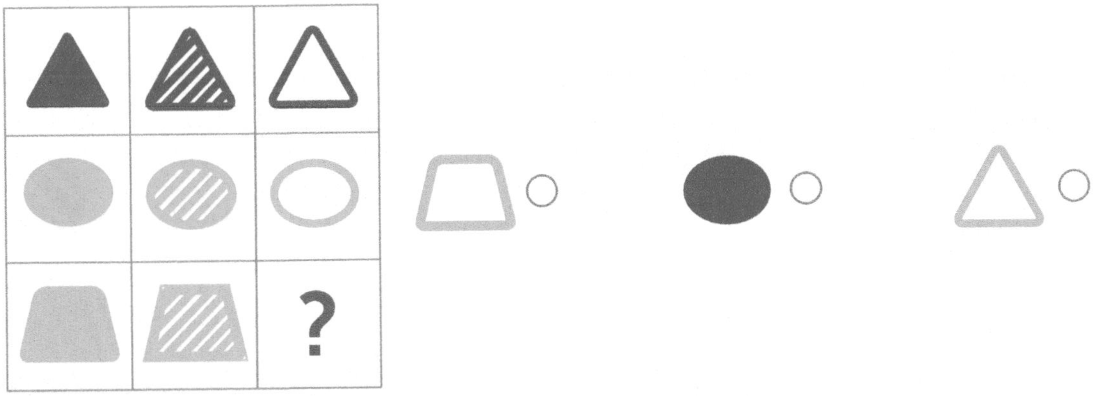

9.

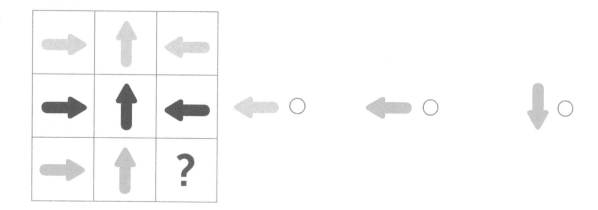

10.

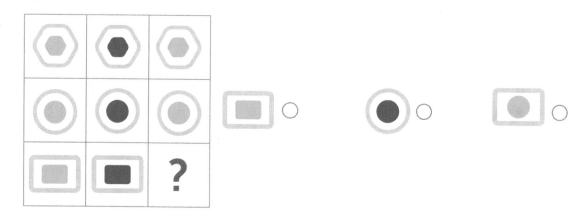

11.

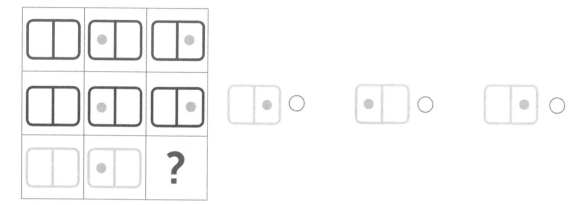

12.

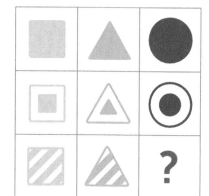

13.

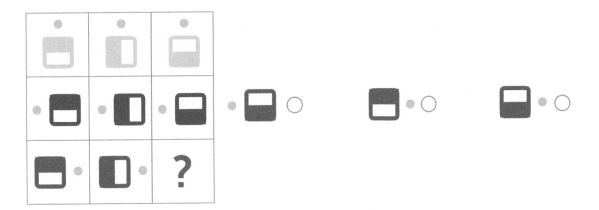

14.

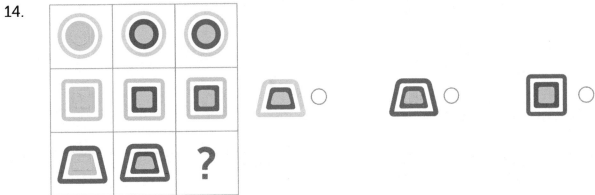

15.

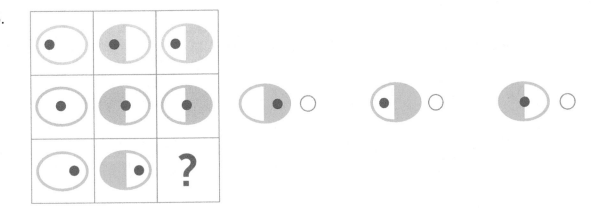

Pattern Matrices

1.

2.

3.

4.

5.

6.

7.

8.

9.

10.

11.

12.

13.

14.

15.

Pattern Completion

Skills Tested: pattern recognition

Foundational Knowledge: colors, patterns

Directions: Which of the answer choices completes the pattern?

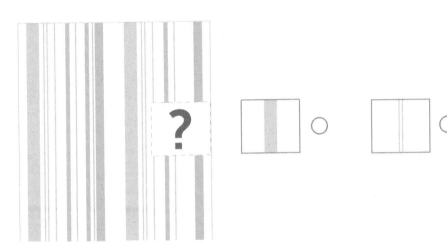

Answer Explanation

Which choice matches the area around the empty box in the pattern?

The third choice is the match because it contains both blue lines and orange lines. (Point to the blue and orange lines in both the pattern and the correct choice.)

Teaching Tips

→ Focus on shared attributes of the area surrounding the empty portion and the correct answer. These may include color, shape, quantity, and size/thickness.

→ Show your student how they can eliminate answer choices. For example, the first two answer options can be easily eliminated because they have no orange.

1.

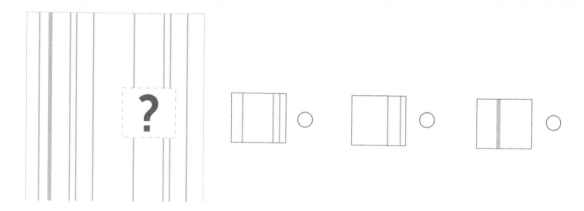

2.

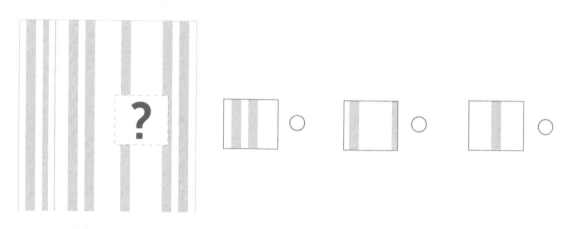

3.

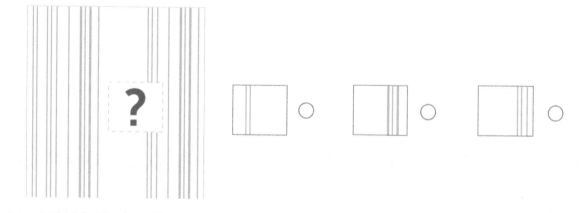

4.

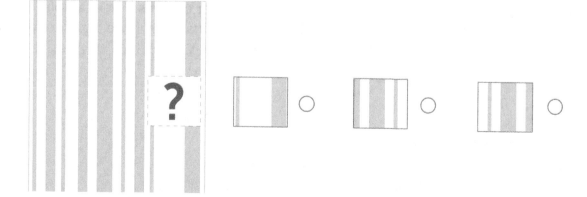

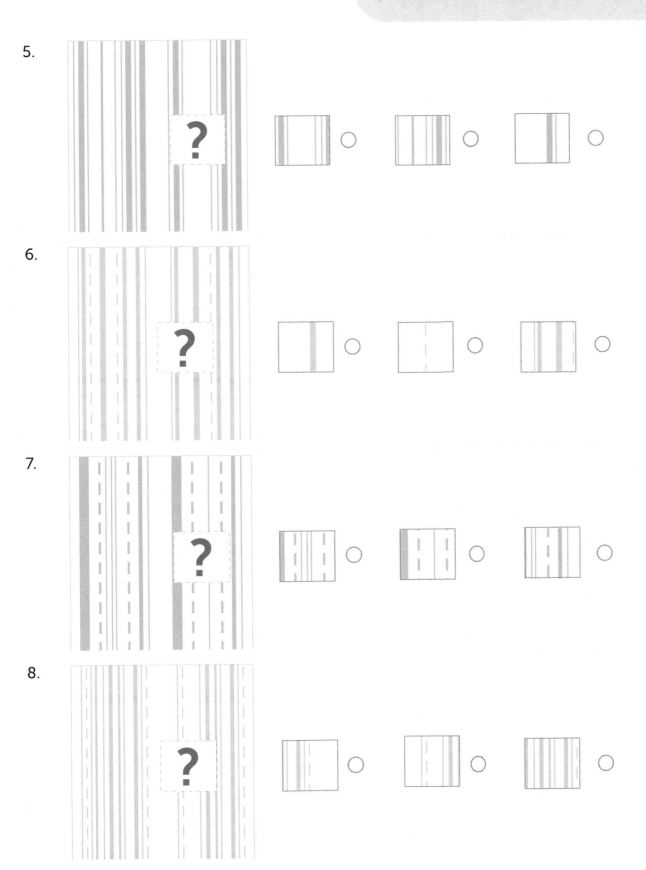

5.

6.

7.

8.

9.

 ○   ○ ○

10.

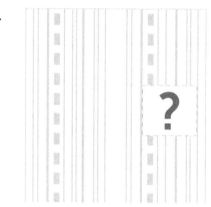   ○ ○ ○

11.

   ○   ○ ○

12.

   ○ ○ ○

13.

 ○ ○ ○

14.

 ○ ○ ○

15.

 ○ ○ ○

Pattern Completion

1.

2.

3.

4.

5.

6.

7.

8.

9.

10.

11.

12.

13.

14.

15.

Directions: Which picture goes in the empty box to complete the pattern?

Answer Explanation

Let's identify the pattern: rectangle, star, trapezoid.

Now the pattern starts again: rectangle.

What comes next?

The star is the next shape in the pattern: rectangle, star, trapezoid, rectangle, star, trapezoid.

Teaching Tips

→ Have your student draw a line where the first pattern ends and the new pattern begins.

→ Extend the pattern for several more boxes so that your student can see that these items are only a "snapshot" or portion of a longer pattern.

1.

2.

3.

4.

5.

○ ○ ○

6.

○ ○ ○

7.

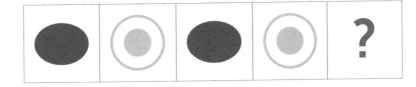

○ ○ ○

8.

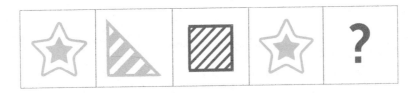

○ ○ ○

9.

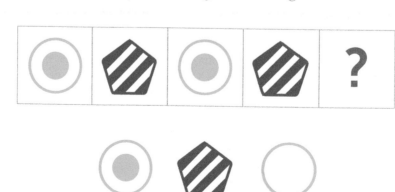

10.

11.

12.

13.

14.

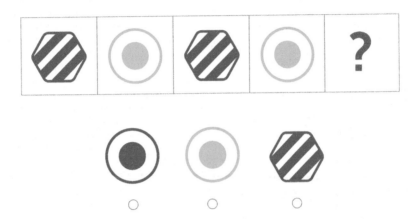

15.

Figure Series

1. The pattern is empty triangle, hexagon, empty triangle, hexagon, ….The next shape is an **empty triangle**.

2. The pattern is circle, square, triangle, circle ….The next shape is a **square**.

3. The pattern is hexagon, star, triangle, hexagon, ….The next shape is a **star**.

4. The pattern is solid square, solid square, star, solid square, …. The next shape is a **solid square**.

5. The pattern is star with thick stripes, rectangle, star with thick stripes, rectangle, ….The next shape is a **star with thick stripes**.

6. The pattern is trapezoid, pentagon, circle, trapezoid, …. The next shape is a **pentagon**.

7. The pattern is oval, circle, oval, circle, ….The next shape is an **oval**.

8. The pattern is star, triangle, square, star, ….The next shape is a **triangle**.

9. The pattern is pentagon, trapezoid, square, pentagon, …. The next shape is a **trapezoid**.

10. The pattern is triangle on the bottom left, triangle on the top right, square, triangle on the bottom left, …. The next shape is a **triangle on the top right**.

11. The pattern is solid square, hexagon, rectangle, solid square, …. The next shape is a **hexagon**.

12. The pattern is a circle within a circle, pentagon, circle within a circle, pentagon, …. **The next shape is a circle within a circle.**

13. The pattern is circle, solid trapezoid, star, circle, …. The next shape is a **solid trapezoid**.

14. The pattern is hexagon, circle, hexagon, circle, …. The next shape is a **hexagon**.

15. The pattern is hexagon within a hexagon, triangle, hexagon within a hexagon, triangle, … The next shape is a **hexagon within a hexagon**.